THE SEVEN WONDERS
OF THE MODERN WORLD

CHRIST
THE REDEEMER

BY ELIZABETH NOLL

BELLWETHER MEDIA • MINNEAPOLIS, MN

Blastoff! Discovery launches a new mission: reading to learn. Filled with facts and features, each book offers you an exciting new world to explore!

BLASTOFF! UNIVERSE

BLASTOFF! Beginners — GRADE K

BLASTOFF! READERS — GRADES 1-3

DISCOVERY — GRADE 4

This edition first published in 2021 by Bellwether Media, Inc.

No part of this publication may be reproduced in whole or in part without written permission of the publisher.
For information regarding permission, write to Bellwether Media, Inc., Attention: Permissions Department, 6012 Blue Circle Drive, Minnetonka, MN 55343.

Library of Congress Cataloging-in-Publication Data

Names: Noll, Elizabeth, author.
Title: Christ the Redeemer / by Elizabeth Noll.
Description: Minneapolis, MN : Bellwether Media, 2021. | Series: Blastoff! Discovery: The seven wonders of the modern world | Includes bibliographical references and index. | Audience: Ages 7-13 | Audience: Grades 4-6 | Summary: "Engaging images accompany information about the Christ the Redeemer statue. The combination of high-interest subject matter and narrative text is intended for students in grades 3 through 8"–Provided by publisher.
Identifiers: LCCN 2020018898 (print) | LCCN 2020018899 (ebook) | ISBN 9781644872666 | ISBN 9781681037295 (ebook)
Subjects: LCSH: (Rio de Janeiro, Brazil)–Juvenile literature. | Rio de Janeiro (Brazil)–Buildings, structures, etc.–Juvenile literature.
Classification: LCC NA9355.R56 N65 2021 (print) | LCC NA9355.R56 (ebook) | DDC 730.981/53–dc23
LC record available at https://lccn.loc.gov/2020018898
LC ebook record available at https://lccn.loc.gov/2020018899

Text copyright © 2021 by Bellwether Media, Inc. BLASTOFF! DISCOVERY and associated logos are trademarks and/or registered trademarks of Bellwether Media, Inc.

Editor: Betsy Rathburn   Designer: Brittany McIntosh

Printed in the United States of America, North Mankato, MN.

TABLE OF CONTENTS

A WARM WELCOME

The plane has finally landed. You are in Rio de Janeiro! You have many adventures planned for your time in Brazil. First, you travel through the city's busy streets to Mount Corcovado. There, you step aboard a train. Buildings and trees flash by as the train climbs the steep mountain.

Finally, you reach the **summit**. The city of Rio is stretched out before you. Its beaches and jungles look tiny from this height. Above you, one of the most famous statues in the world stretches high into the air. The wide arms of Christ the Redeemer welcome you to Rio!

THE MAN ON THE MOUNTAIN

Christ the Redeemer is a statue of Jesus Christ, the central figure of the Christian religion. The statue stands on Mount Corcovado, which rises 2,310 feet (704 meters) above the city of Rio de Janeiro.

MOUNT CORCOVADO

THINK ABOUT IT

Why do you think Christ the Redeemer was built on Mount Corcovado?

From this height, visitors can see other rock formations rising above the Atlantic Ocean. The skyscrapers of Rio's busy city center are also in view. Closer to the mountain, **favelas** look like they are stacked one on top the other. Every day, thousands of visitors take in this view.

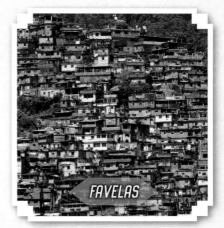

FAVELAS

WHERE IS CHRIST THE REDEEMER?

CHRIST THE REDEEMER
RIO DE JANEIRO, BRAZIL

N
W   E
S

Christ the Redeemer stands 125 feet (38 meters) tall from the base of the **pedestal**. The statue's outstretched arms measure 92 feet (28 meters) from fingertip to fingertip. Many think the pose looks like a hug. It is often viewed as a friendly welcome to Rio!

The statue is covered in thousands of tiny tiles. These triangles of soapstone form a **mosaic** that covers the statue from head to toe. Underneath the tiles is a frame of concrete and steel.

The statue sits atop an eight-sided pedestal. The pedestal rises 26 feet (8 meters) tall. It includes a small **chapel** where visitors can pray. Nearby, there are restaurants that serve hungry **tourists**.

MANY ARTISTS, ONE SCULPTURE

In 1922, Brazil celebrated the 100th anniversary of its **independence** from Portugal. Many people threw parties. There was even a **World Expo** to celebrate. More than 10 countries attended!

EXPO 2019

The World Expo has been held around the world since the 1800s. In 2019, a gardening expo was held in Beijing, China. It was the world's biggest gardening show!

THINK ABOUT IT

People build statues to remember a special person or event. If you could build a giant statue, who or what would it be? Why?

MOUNT CORCOVADO BEFORE CHRIST THE REDEEMER WAS BUILT

But some people wanted to do more. The previous year, the **archdiocese** of Rio asked for permission from Brazil's government to build a large statue of Jesus. The statue was meant to be a **symbol** of hope and comfort. Permission was granted! The **foundation** was laid on April 4, 1922. But there was still work to be done.

HEITOR DA SILVA COSTA

ORIGINAL DESIGN

A competition was held to choose an **engineer**. Heitor da Silva Costa won the job! His sketches showed Jesus holding a cross in one hand and the world in the other. But some people did not like this idea. A sculptor, Carlos Oswald, made a new design. The new statue was standing with its arms open wide. People loved it!

Many artists worked together on the statue. A sculptor named Paul Landowski formed a **model** of the statue. He hired Gheorghe Leonida to make the statue's face. The model was taken to Brazil, where it would be recreated in a stronger material.

GHEORGHE LEONIDA WITH THE STATUE'S HEAD

PAUL LANDOWSKI

ART OLYMPICS

Paul Landowski won a gold medal at the 1928 Summer Olympics. That year, artists competed to make art related to sports!

CHRIST THE REDEEMER
UNDER CONSTRUCTION

Designers had to figure out how to make the statue as strong as possible. They decided to use **reinforced** concrete. Workers used a railroad to bring materials up Mount Corcovado. They hauled water in from a fountain near the construction site. This helped them make concrete on top of the mountain.

The concrete was poured into **molds** created from the clay models. Bars of steel were inserted to make the concrete stronger. **Scaffolding** helped workers stack the concrete pieces on the pedestal. When all of the pieces were in place, it was time to finish the statue.

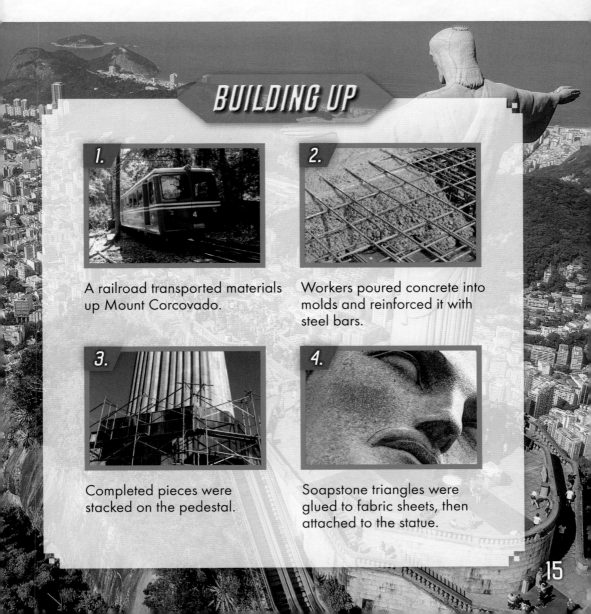

BUILDING UP

1.
A railroad transported materials up Mount Corcovado.

2.
Workers poured concrete into molds and reinforced it with steel bars.

3.
Completed pieces were stacked on the pedestal.

4.
Soapstone triangles were glued to fabric sheets, then attached to the statue.

On a visit to France, Heitor da Silva Costa saw a fountain lined with tiles. This gave him an idea. He decided to cover the statue with tiles. The tiles would be tiny, polished pieces of soapstone.

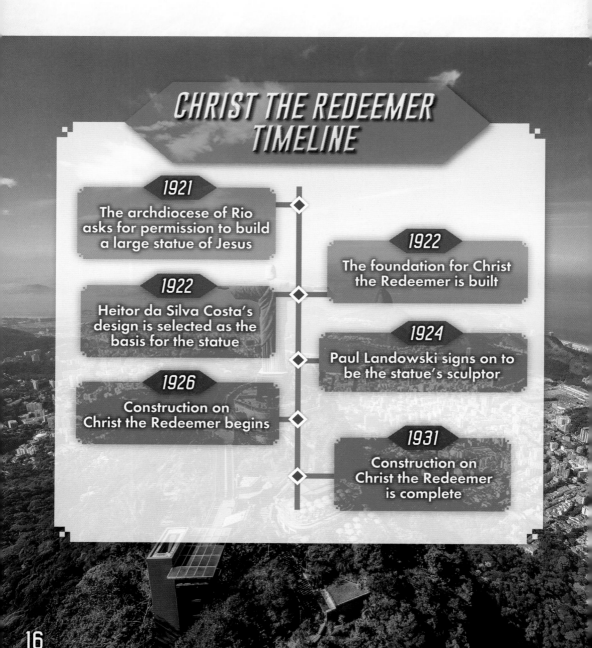

CHRIST THE REDEEMER TIMELINE

1921
The archdiocese of Rio asks for permission to build a large statue of Jesus

1922
The foundation for Christ the Redeemer is built

1922
Heitor da Silva Costa's design is selected as the basis for the statue

1924
Paul Landowski signs on to be the statue's sculptor

1926
Construction on Christ the Redeemer begins

1931
Construction on Christ the Redeemer is complete

Each triangle-shaped tile is about 1 inch (2.5 centimeters) across. It took millions of tiny tiles to cover the entire statue. Women who lived near the statue worked on the tile project. They glued the tiny tiles to big pieces of fabric. Then, the fabric pieces were attached to the statue. The statue was completed in 1931.

Over the years, Christ the Redeemer has undergone many changes. In 2003, construction started on a series of walkways and elevators. In 2006, a chapel was built inside the pedestal. This allowed people to worship at the statue. It is a single room with chairs and a marble **altar**.

In 2011, bright lights were added to make the statue more visible from far away. A few years later, new **lightning rods** on the fingers and head were added to protect the statue against storms.

CHAPEL

The statue faces challenges, too. Over many years, dirt and mold build up and need to be cleaned. But soap and other chemicals can damage the statue. Instead, it is cleaned with gentle **sandblasting**.

SANDBLASTING

The statue is also in danger from **vandalism**. In 2010, people climbed scaffolding to spray-paint the statue. Many around Brazil were upset. Rio's mayor called the act a crime against the nation. Those responsible soon turned themselves in. The paint was removed after a few days of cleaning.

The weather also puts Christ the Redeemer at risk. Wind and lightning cause damage to the statue's tiles. They must be replaced. When the statue was built, the tile came from soapstone **quarries** about 250 miles (402 kilometers) from Rio. But today, the quarries are empty. No other quarry has the same soapstone used to build the statue.

Instead, new tiles must be made out of a different soapstone. During every repair, some of the original tiles are replaced with new, darker tiles. Eventually, the entire statue will be a new color!

THEN AND NOW

THEN

For more than 70 years, visitors had to walk up 220 steps to get to Christ the Redeemer!

NOW

In the early 2000s, escalators were installed. They allow people to visit the statue much more easily!

A SYMBOL FOR MANY

Today, Christ the Redeemer is still a powerful symbol for many around the world. The statue has millions of visitors every year. In 2007, it was named a Wonder of the Modern World. The number of visitors grew!

Famous people often visit the statue. In 1980, Pope John Paul II gave a speech at the base of the statue. In 2011, President Barack Obama visited the statue with his family. Actor and songwriter Queen Latifah visited in 2015. In 2018, Princess Mako of Japan visited.

PRESIDENT OBAMA AND FAMILY

24

Christ the Redeemer often serves as a backdrop for events in the city. For example, the 2016 Summer Olympics were held in Rio. Thousands of people flooded the city. The Olympic torch was blessed at the statue before the games began.

The statue is often featured in movies and TV shows. It was in the 2011 movie *Fast Five*. It was also featured in "That Hug," a popular song by Gilberto Gil. Christ the Redeemer is a popular symbol of Brazil!

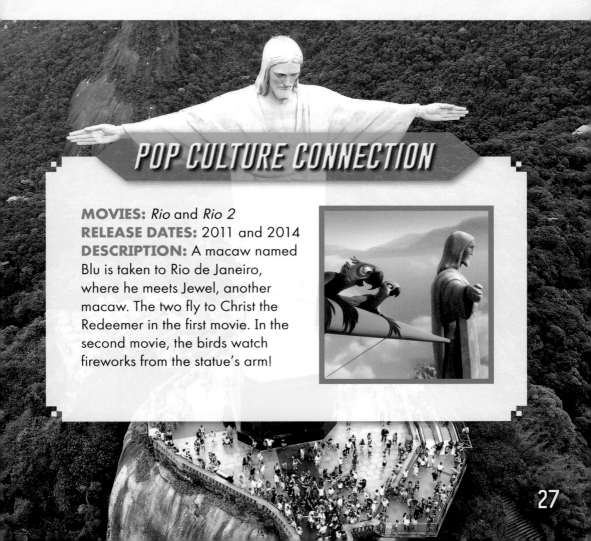

POP CULTURE CONNECTION

MOVIES: *Rio* and *Rio 2*
RELEASE DATES: 2011 and 2014
DESCRIPTION: A macaw named Blu is taken to Rio de Janeiro, where he meets Jewel, another macaw. The two fly to Christ the Redeemer in the first movie. In the second movie, the birds watch fireworks from the statue's arm!

Christ the Redeemer does not just represent Brazil. It also brings peace to many people around the world. During the 2020 coronavirus **pandemic**, the statue was lit with messages of hope. Christ the Redeemer is a symbol for Christians, the city of Rio, and the entire country of Brazil!

COMPARE AND CONTRAST

CHRIST THE REDEEMER

STATUE OF LIBERTY

LOCATION	**LOCATION**
Rio de Janeiro, Brazil	New York Ciy, United States
YEAR COMPLETED	**YEAR COMPLETED**
1931	1886
HEIGHT	**HEIGHT**
125 feet (38 meters)	305 feet (93 meters)
WEIGHT	**WEIGHT**
1,145 tons (1,038 metric tons)	225 tons (204 metric tons)
MATERIALS	**MATERIALS**
reinforced concrete, soapstone	iron, copper

Christ the Redeemer was built to last a long time. But even strong materials like concrete and stone can crumble. The people of Brazil clean and repair it when it gets damaged. Their care will keep Christ the Redeemer watching over Rio for years to come!

GLOSSARY

altar—a raised table used for worship in a religious setting

archdiocese—an area that an archbishop is in charge of; an archbishop is a religious leader.

chapel—a small building where religious worship happens

engineer—a person who designs things to be built

favelas—areas of crowded, run-down housing on the outskirts of Brazil's cities

foundation—a base or support on top of which a structure is built

independence—freedom from the control of someone or something

lightning rods—long pieces of metal used to attract lightning away from a building or other structure

model—a small figure of something to be built

molds—empty spaces into which concrete, clay, or another substance is poured to create certain shapes

mosaic—a decoration or artwork made from many tiles

pandemic—an event in which an illness spreads over a large area to many people

pedestal—the base a statue stands on

quarries—places from which rocks are dug for use in building

reinforced—made stronger with added materials

sandblasting—the process of shooting sand at an object to clean it

scaffolding—a series of raised platforms, or scaffolds, built as support for workers and their tools and materials

summit—the highest point of a mountain

symbol—something that stands for something else

tourists—people who travel to visit a place

vandalism—intentional damage

World Expo—a large event that showcases the achievements of different nations

TO LEARN MORE

AT THE LIBRARY

Gitlin, Marty. *Brazil*. Minneapolis, Minn.: Bellwether Media, 2018.

Jackson, Tom. *Wonders of the World*. New York, N.Y.: DK Publishing, 2014.

Spilsbury, Louise. *Brazil and Rio de Janeiro*. London, U.K.: Franklin Watts, 2016.

ON THE WEB

FACTSURFER

Factsurfer.com gives you a safe, fun way to find more information.

1. Go to www.factsurfer.com.

2. Enter "Christ the Redeemer" into the search box and click 🔍.

3. Select your book cover to see a list of related content.

INDEX